Oceans of My Soul

Oceans of My Soul

Solo Sailing Under a Tropical Sky

Gillie Davies

Dedication

This is dedicated to my lifelong friend, Helen, who has supported me throughout the last 30 odd years as a best friend, confident and holiday companion. Thank you . x

The glittery pink beauty who stands before the world

belies the powerful woman you are

your strength of character

professionally calm countenance

cannot hide the passion that smoulders within

you inspire so many with your bravery

in facing challenges alone

yet striding forward and owning your space

you are a guiding beacon of feminine grace

with strength in love and gentleness

so much elegance in your compassion

my beautiful amazing siren sister

I am blessed that we call each other friend

Forward

This is the third in the series Oceans of My Soul. By now I had planned to have crossed the Indian Ocean, however, cancer and Covid 19 got in the way. I have moved to Phuket, Thailand as I had some critical boat issues that have also delayed my departure for Africa, and I am getting those critical repairs done here.

I'm not sad about any of these "setbacks", they are as much a part of my journey as my poems are. There was a time, when the words I once had, almost got lost in the depth of it all, but I trusted that I would find them again or perhaps that they would find me and here we are. In a post pandemic fundamentally changed world, I am grateful for the words that come, for the inspirations I get from the people I meet and those who support me.

Someone asked me 'why does sailing and poetry go together and how did you become a poet sailor?' Those of you who have read my first 2 books will have an inkling and I would add that the rhythm of the tides, sea, winds, and currents which are governed by the moon, and determine much of the sailing experience, lend themselves to the rhythms of poetry, even when they are in free writing form as many of mine are. I find the oceans and the creatures in and above them have a poetry of their own and I cannot help to be inspired by them as so many other poets are.

Thank you for purchasing this book which helps to keep me from your door with a begging bowl! It enables me to keep my beautiful boat Tuppenny afloat and gives those who support me a bit of a respite! It also means that I get to share some of my life with you in a very intimate way.

If you should ever spy me in an anchorage or perhaps landing my dinghy on the beach, come by, say hello, it would be good to meet you. If you feel like getting in touch, I look forward to hearing from you at gilliesailssolo@gmail.com If you sail past me on your way somewhere, do give me a wave or call on channel 16! My website is www.gilliesailssolo.com I also have Instagram, Facebook and Twitter pages.

Cheers for now, I'll see you when I'm looking at you!

Ocean of Solitude

There is a joy

deep in my veins

as my tide recedes the shore

there is a longing

for the peace

in an Ocean of Solitude

Gillie Davies

I Write

As I write

I let go those past mistakes

leave them flowing on the page

trying to make sense of a journey

that defies explanation

As the words form

in the darkness of small hours

driving like the rain

from a tropical sky

torrential

unforgiving

Now they seep

into every pour of my skin

blistering under the heat of the sun

at times their ferocity of feelings

take the breath from my lungs

gasping

I spit them across the page

of my life

You Are Home

Oh my dear

every time love leaves your heart

your soul gathers strength

until one day

just like a miracle

you look yourself in the eye

knowing all the love you ever needed

was here inside you all along

then

you are home

Celebrating

I am going to celebrate who I am

that passionately emotional creature

who loves with every ounce of her being.....

who knows that the storm is coming

and who howls at the moon

because she knows her very emotional passion

will hurt like hell again and again and again

Gillie Davies

The Wrong Side

On the wrong side of yesterday

how could I have known

that the right side of tomorrow

might have given me this

all the perfect todays of you

Will You

Will you come tonight

after the darkness arrives

tie up to my side

set me alight with a touch

give me your soul

show me how you feel

be with me til dawn

kiss my lips in tender release

trace fingers into secret places

delve beneath the facade

make love to me

so that I can know

you are worth waiting for

Gillie Davies

Love Yourself Quietly

Try loving yourself quietly

you cannot change others

walk in your own light

others may or may not see it

those who do will encourage you to shine

those who don't will be in shadows

left behind in the wake of the energy

you share with the world

as you dance yourself through life

Symphonic Steps

Sometimes you find a someone

who turns the music of your soul

into the sweetest serenade

yet when they leave

the music dies for a while

Let your music come from your own love

from the beauty of the world around

the majesty of the mighty mountain

the ferocity of the winter winds

from the high call of the lone sea eagle

it is then my darling

you will carry a symphony in every step

rather than losing your

music in the steps of another

I see

I can see from here

the outline of the muscles on your chest

and I long to touch you

to be the beauty I am in my head and heart

stroking you and feeling the strength in your core

you don't know I see

how you stand in your private moments

reflecting on the things you've done

the hearts you've broken

those smiles you tore from another's face

with your betrayal and meanness

and how I long to find that softness in your belly

where your small creature lives

hidden away from the world

those fears and uncertainties you locked in a box

are just waiting

for your moments of vulnerability

then I'll have the key

twist it swiftly in the lock and bam!

You'll be knocked out of kilter

I can see you still

now searching for the why's

trying to reason it all with your self-recriminations

diluting your actions with fictitious justifications

did you bring this on yourself?

No! surely your motives were clear

and better to be honest right?

except you weren't were you

your honesty came with lust

which is such a sweet talker

such a smooth subtle shifter

a player in the game of self-gratification

disguising itself as a heart bursting with

the joy of love

rather than the groin of desire and

self-serving want

all this I know about you

your truths and your lies

yet still I long to hold you in the sepia image

and rest my head in the beauty of your body

Illusions

Illusions of freedom

fill the lens

strong inspiring words

drift out on the horizon

where hope lies waiting

yet she is wingless

just as our prison is without walls

Gillie Davies

The Happiest Man

Speak to me a story

a beautiful one

where you find the light is perfect for a photograph

where the laughter from your children

causes a single tear

when the breath on the breeze smells of frangipani

so as to whisk away any thought of care

a moon glow dusts off the shelves of anguish

you can be for one enthralling moment

the happiest man

and I can feel your joy course through my soul

Not Here

I love you so much it hurts to think of you

there and not here

it hurts not to hold you and be held by you

and yet

the thought of you

your face

that smile

is so uplifting

that it gives me hope

and that hope lifts my entire day

Gillie Davies

Wretched

Sometimes the wretchedness tears at

the fine fabric of my soul

leaving me bereft

filthy as the muddy silt waters of the tidal river

sludge is a heavy burden of hurt

covering the last glimmers of hope

Protection

The veil of stormy thoughts lifts

and even if the fear felt real

the sun was always shining

behind the clouds of doubt

The protection you seek is within you

it has always been so

the stars are in your veins my darling

they will never let you go

Gillie Davies

Tumbled

I tumbled backwards in the dark

not knowing where I would fall

I do it all by myself

in the moments of aloneness

where I begin to dream

of what might be

in all it's improbabilities

and I landed there

hoping it was your heart

what a fool to think

you would catch me there

when to you it shows weakness

to me it shows courage

Triumphant Queen

It's on this morning

with the sun painting the mountain pink

she sheds the skin

that made her sink

sloughs the old

puts on the new

in vivid colours of every hue

the most exquisite she has yet been

to rise again a triumphant queen

Quiet Solitude

Cupping your cheeks in my hands

looking at you

deep pools of brown coffee eyes

sucking me in

the smile does it

transports me to that other place

our place of quiet solitude

just simply darling

I think

I want to say

I love you

Crossing Minds

As the last light

leaves today's sky

and we hurtle headlong

into our tomorrow

I wonder for the umpteenth time

if I even crossed your mind

and wish to god

you didn't fill mine

Gillie Davies

Dandelion

Maybe I'll be like the dandelion seed

blown in the wind

lost forever in a dream

a tiny seed of worthlessness

who's touch is imperceptible

to the rocks and pebbles

yet who in time

takes root and blooms

into the brightest sun glow

My Adventurous Ride

Wanted to write

had an engine to fix

from dawn til gone six

diesel in my mix

can't trust my emotions

need my boat on the ocean

I'll get there I'm sure

just need to work for the cure

then the thunder and lightening

can make it quite frightening

with the boat on her side

with the rip of the tide

I just have to hang on

with a tack or a gybe

always the captain

to my adventurous ride

Roots

Letting someone leave is so hard

the pain can last a while

then slowly

almost imperceptibly

you start to deepen your own roots

start climbing

your thoughts and eyes skyward

'til before long

you have emerged into a whole new world

Dare

Should I dare
to let you know the me of me

Would you care
or break my heart and squander me

Can you hear
the way I'm falling through the cracks

Do you know
for me there's no way back

I cannot know why this should be
a longing an eternity

The twist of fate may yet reveal
your deftness and your sex appeal

Gillie Davies

Endless Possibilities

Don't linger there too long friend

or get too comfortable in sorrow

allow the pain to light a fire in your blood

to rise up

take flight

changing heartbreak into endless possibilities

Imperceptible Moments

Swallows at the mast head

call to the world

announcing the arrival of the Sun

tides meander in the peace of the predawn

ever changing

yet remaining the same

each imperceptible moment can be lost

unless I stop to listen to the silence

making peace with itself

Petals from the Rose

I watch your seduction

behind an unseen veil

precision timing operation

you're like a carefree spirit

until the final flight

your turns and intricacies unmatched

landing is perfect

just at the right moment

throttle back

wing flaps down

so smooth a touchdown

that she is unaware

she is already yours

taxiing down her runway

impression of certain re-flight

but that was never

your intention

as you finally come to a standstill

power down your engines

she all but falls at your feet

like the petals from a rose

Hard Shell

Is it wrapped around your heart

do you know how it grew there

is there a place where it opens

are you longing for it to split apart

to allow the soul of you

to flow into the world

to be known

seen

heard

did it cause you to fall

along the road of your youth

will you open it now

and rejoice

This Troubled Road

Oh! My brother

I'll walk with you on this troubled road

yet hear the news with agitation

and I would say stand firm

keep hold

we will not buckle

nor will we fold

The path is long

and dusty motes will suck

all love and care from your breast

but we'll be firm and standing strong

we will smite the silent foe

Then gently

as a flame that flickers

in the cold and dark of night

we will see life's new path glisten

and follow it with all our might

And on that path I'll tread beside you
hand in hand with purpose clear
we will reach that gleaming treasure
and once again will conquer fear

Getting the Hang of It!

Getting the hang of just

being me

for me

is my new anchorage

in life's voyage

and I am loving life

I'm being reinvented

with constant adventures

and this is my time and place to be

in the exhilaration of my bliss

I fill my blank pages

with a joy that is my own

On My Watch

Watch me change on my watch

this sea gypsy

as she sails the seas

a nomad on the ocean

who's direction is determined

by wind and tide

moon and stars

I belong here

in this moment

where I move with time

on waters that carry me

along a journey

where I meet

the me-ness of me

which becomes one

with the rhythm of the earth and oceans wide

Gillie Davies

Your Words

Your words paint

tear stains

down my soul

Your song

drives nails

into my heart

Your love

injects poison

into my veins

My feet

drag me screaming

from your abyss

Belonging Begins

Stepping out into the morning

sleep laden eyes adjusting

water buffalo enjoying dew heavy grass

elegant egrets follow in compliment

a huddling of fishing boats await darker nights

some long-forgotten dreams lie rotting in harbour

whilst living ones bob gently in the bay

and the birds call to announce the day

I counted more than twenty different sounds

here is where belonging begins

where my horizon stretches out across

oceans of ideas

Gillie Davies

Igbo Warrior

There you stood

tall

strong

lithe

my Igbo Warrior

oh how I loved you

There you fought

tribal

brotherhood

unwavering

my Igbo warrior

oh how I needed you

There you starved

beaten

defiant

smouldering

my Igbo warrior

oh how I held you

Now rise again

rejuvenated

powerful

majestic

my Igbo warrior

save your beloved Biafraland

for oh! how she loves you

Gillie Davies

Knife Edge

Balanced on knife edge

of emotional turmoil

diving headlong into

a story of my own making

falling in I understand

empowerment is mine

if I take it

sloughing off the fear

leaping joyfully into the present

On this edge

between the bliss and the abyss

adventure and tedium

each has their own pitfalls

the sink or swim variety

wondering how to get through

yet the alternative of solid ground

a slow death and treadmill to hell

Standing here looking

between the two choices

opting for strong tides and wide oceans

sails aloft hoping to reach

the far shore of this life

Gillie Davies

Carved in Stone

Darling

don't linger too long

in that heart of comfort

for she is a fickle friend

luring you into that false place

where you feel you belong

You have no business here

where love lives

it is not your home

not a place to rest your weary bones

you must move on

for she will break your heart

and then carve your soul in stone!

Loud Silence

The silence is loud in my soul

it screams with passion

my sorrow

and flows so effortlessly through me

there is a comfort there

in the cushion of woe

It takes me on the current

to new places I haven't yet dared to go

I will lean into this gift

take time to feel the peace it creates

and I'll drift on the breeze

to a familiar space

that I'll call

home

Black Dog

Looking at my photograph

it seems to me quite clear

I need to do some ironing

and not just what I wear!

The cheeks the arms and midriff

could do with liposuction

whilst lifting could be possible

don't want to breath from belly button!

Reminding myself quite firmly

I need to act my age

I write another line of thoughts

and deftly turn the page

The jobs I had to do today

stay critically not done

and once again I'll kick myself

tonight when day is gone

But keeping myself cheerful
not allowing fear to grip me
with chastisements of my laziness
is really not that easy!

So I'll write another poem
fill the dink and go ashore
I'll lunch out with my buddy
instead of doing bloody chores

Then when I get home later
I'll pen a few lines more
Black Dog he wont be with me
he'll stay chained upon the shore!

Sailing On

Well it's three am
and its hot outside
and I wonder what
you did tonight
where the wild winds blow
and the snow falls fast
can you dare to dream
of our days now past

sailing on
sailing on
gotta keep on
sailing on

So I stumble out
to the starry night
and I'm watching out
for that fire light
that once flamed high in your blue eyes
but I can't quite catch it
before it dies

sailing on

sailing on

gotta keep on

sailing on

Did you ever wish

you were here with me

on our little boat

sailing the seven seas

where we sang our songs

and made the wildest schemes

of togetherness

until the end of dreams

sailing on

sailing on

I just keep on

sailing on

Gillie Davies

Motorbike Adventure

Tell me your story

that time when

out on a limb

you took flight

and traversed two continents

on two wheels with revving engines

and the wind

that nearly blew you over

the tiredness

of dropped 100kg bikes

for the umpteenth time

broken panniers and legs

bruises that lasted for weeks

of unknown days

barely remembered moments

of no plan

of 'I don't know!' answers

here's where adventures are

under the bright milky way

in foreign lands

where language of security is an unknown concept

and the 'Where are you going?'

is answered with

'South'

when the

'when will you be back'

is another

'I don't know'

these are the times of your life

and mine

these are the times I want to feel

those smells and colours

the heat and cold to your bones moments

those desperate times when you thought

'I can't'

but you did

and here you are

in another adventure

another lifetime

telling and listening to

our stories of the

time when

real life began

and we knew the meaning of

living in the moment because of all those

'I don't know' answers

we gave to the

stay at homes and

holiday makers

who can't grasp a shred of

reasoning

because there is none here in these tellings

these are the adventures and life

that we were put here

just to live

Magic

Find a quiet spot to anchor

away from the bustle

and busyness

lie back on the deck

and watch the stars pop out

that is when the Magic happens

Gillie Davies

Constellations of My Youth

I will trudge this dusty road

to the constellations of my youth

where my essence emerged

in an explosion of stardust

to be blown by unseen winds

through the universe and to hang

suspended in a moon beam

There are stories at the end of this road

speaking only of beginnings

of youthful ideas older than time

where hope and new opportunity

spins in a glitter of light and colour

it's there for the oldest of souls

who toil on our small dust particle

watched by unseen beings

as we too watch them

marvelling at each other's beauty and grace

Picture

Picture the singing bird

with yellow breast

and a sunny tune

he calls where creativity

and wealth of not knowing rest

in between leaves of opportunity

which blow in the breezes of ideas

and drift high up to the light

landing gently as a seed

on the fertile soil

of an inner garden of peace

Lost

Stealthy like creeping ivy

a little tentacle here

a searching strand of vine with the tiniest leaf

but it's taking hold under the surface

unnoticed

wrapping itself around you

until suddenly it seems

without warning you can't breathe

gasping you try to make it to the surface

but you're sinking fast

into the blackness

the dark fog

all consuming

then you can no longer choose what to do next

driving from one place to another

but don't stop

return yet drive past

but don't know why

wander around aimlessly

searching the shelves as if you've lost something

yet not knowing what

ahh an appointment that was it

pick up things and put them in the basket of time

pay the piper

pick up laundry

collect the cat

yet know there is something

forgotten

get home and climb aboard

allow the salty tsunami waterfall down your face

not even knowing why the floor

has disappeared from beneath your feet

Gillie Davies

Girl with the Heart Balloon

Pictures painted on a wall
social statements to enthral
drawn to feed the weary minds
telling truths we left behind

Now on canvas all en-framed
auction hammers well maintained
bought by someone rich and noble
price is paid belies the trouble
shreds of paper in the frame
hope it's thought to defame

Human minds cannot be fathomed
now commands a higher ransom
millions paid for ink on canvas
cannot see how society stands this
thousands die for need of food
feels the art is forged in blood

Celebrates the spoilt few

who can't see clearly for the view

one small child reaching up

balloon of heart she wants to grasp

the simple things of life unfold

stories on life's wall are told

Joyful

Be joyful in your Soul

push away the constant criticism of your mind

do something great for you

be not critical

then my darling

you will achieve something immeasurable

that will carry you to the top of that hill

which you have climbed for so long

Drift

In the late afternoon

just before the sun sinks

behind the majestic mountains to the West

I watch as the diamonds

glisten and dance on the water

a priceless array of jewels

shining just for me

as my boat rocks

gently in the ebbing tide

and the warm breeze

lifts the flag of courtesy

to flutter aloft

birds call cicadas still not chirping

and hail the afternoon

as the coolness returns

and I drift in and out of dreams

Biggest Wonder

Your head rests in my hand

as you sleep

with the other I stroke you

for comfort

mine

soothing and smoothing my mood

into a tranquillity where

thoughts drift into space

a spec on a spec on a spec someone

said in a podcast

that's the wonder of it

that we are here at all

and to know we are

Is the biggest wonder of all

Gratitude

Put those life lessons and hurts into your museum

to visit from time to time

watching how you feel in the nostalgia of them

take the calm poise from beyond

watch how it blooms in your inner garden

Let the gratitude you wash yourself in

keep the joys and laughter

the good ways of your path

flowing like a river

back to your soul

allow it to fill your golden cup

Then

with the generosity of those feelings

allow yourself to share that beauty

with those who tread a solemn path

those who need the love from this nectar

and be glad

Gillie Davies

Plentiful Cups

As the swallow flies aloft

sweet sounds breaking through

the chains of sorrow

which bind my mind

on a bed of self decay

From plentiful cups

I can sip the nectar

to bring nourishment to my soul

What is it that I drink?

just love

it is love

that is the food on my table

LOVE

Fragments of a Life

On these pages

sit little notes

ideas

thoughts

of love to me

Nuggets of inspirations

fragments of joys

glued together like paper-chains

strung out across meadows

freshly laundered for you to watch

Bringing a tear

or a memory

maybe a small smile

of knowing or hope

Gillie Davies

Spring

Here she comes so boisterous

in her iridescent greens

unfolding into a new growth

leaping forth toward the warmth

urging us to be bold

in our appreciation of new birth

Unique Joy

Let the laughter in your belly

spill out into the world

to allow everyone to hear

their own unique joy in space

let it beribbon their day and yours

with such a lightness of mood

to lift all sorrows

just like the early call of the Kingfisher at dawn

Gillie Davies

Reinvention

Selfishly reinvent yourself each day

dance in the shadows of the past

until they fade

into the music of a renewed soul

Touch the stars of all your potential

whilst listening to the rhythms

from the depth of your being

This is the reason you are here

where you truly belong

to paint this new melody loud

with movements of acceptance

overflowing with the joy of your beautiful self

Stand naked in the rains of your malaise

allow the coolness wash

worries from your shoulders

releasing tension with

refreshing relinquishing

This my friend is your only business

this is your life's work

until your inner smile lights up the world

Here's the Thing

Here's the thing

many beautiful souls say

"You're not alone"

but the truth is

I am alone

however

 I am good with that

and honestly

we all need to be

good and comfortable with that aloneness

Storm Clouds

When the storm clouds gather

from your foolish games

then you run headlong towards change

you chase your stars

reinvent your lies

all to be loved by the few

Did you never know

or reason why

the rain and thunder follow you

wrapped around you like a shroud

kissed by your reckless nonchalance

Gillie Davies

Call Him Out

If you take the risk

speak up about what is to you

morally right and just

you will at some stage

have your emotional stability questioned

by a man

because you are a woman

who dared to say your truth

and, as you did that

you called him out

on his own hypocrisy

Of course he will publicly deny it

and will tell of how he

supports women in so many ways

in so doing

he intends to compound his ideas

of your emotional vagrancies

He will be offended

cry foul play

and try once again to discredit you

he will speak to you in private

pleading his case

and publicly say that an offence

was found where none was intended

Darling one

take that risk anyway

speak up

stand up

call him out

it is always worth it

Jigsaw of Life

I have collected on this journey

things

whole and broken

used and discarded

people

lost or asleep

wild and unruly

they have become momentary joys

disappointments

and annoyances

they are the jigsaw of my life

and piece by magical piece

they slip quietly

or loudly into place

to enrich an already abundant soul

with their own style of music

and rhythm

coloured by individual unique paints

bleeding into each other

dusting the canvas with every hue

and although I've walked on

I've carried small particles of them with me

each mote becoming an integral part

of the me that I am

Becoming Powerful

Where is my power

in knowing my vulnerability

or perhaps in my blank pages

allowing me to see

new ideas spread like ink across my being

maybe in my quietness

when I just look out at the world

and say

ahh! there you are

here I am

this woman I am becoming

Belong

Can I truly belong here

holding myself tall in a moment

structuring my life into something meaningful

whole in my dream of life

precious to me and my love of adventure

I am being

right now

in this moment

and I'm complete

I can sense change

looking carefully

deeply to my bones

there's a strength

a fearlessness

Diverted Storm

Storm diverted from the hood

battened down hatches tight and good

hoisted dinghy

lashed to the rail

just hoped it was rain

none of that hail

tucked up tight

and prepped to be swamped

now it looks like it's already dumped

might just get a gust or a sigh

but looks as though it's passed us by!

Ghosting

I met a man

or thought I did

we talked a while

but then he hid

I was light-hearted

nothing heavy

turns out I think

he wasn't ready

I'm strong I know

and sometimes scary

I laugh too loud

perhaps a bit lairy

can be intense

but ghosting?

really?

it makes no sense

just tell me straight

look me in the eye

I really don't mind

just say good bye!

Gillie Davies

Respite

If I request from you

a shadow to cover my head

to shade the hermit from

the glare of judgement and self-doubt

I may not be so defensive in my words

will you give me

a cool place of respite

calling me away peacefully

to the inner sanctuary

allowing me to let the leaving happen

Whisper

Let the smile in your soul

spread across your beautiful face

each time you remember me

and I will whisper your name

across the oceans

on the breeze

Gillie Davies

Lonely Chair

Some days

by the time the sun sets

I am more than weary

loneliness is not a feeling

it's a place where I have my own chair

It's a full wing-backed affair now

I've been a visitor so often

always trying just

to be a guest

but life has

a way of taking you home

Don't you think?

Yet

here's the thing

that chair is becoming comfortable

so maybe I'll sit a while

and just be me

in my lonely chair

Last Breath

Look back along the road

I can tell you my stories

they're not better than yours

I know what I know

will learn what I need to survive

its not the same lesson as you

yet neither's truth

is any more valid than the others'

under one sun we trudge

or skip along until we

take our last breath

Chapters & Pages

New chapters and blank pages

open our minds to adventures

where we meet the friends

we do not yet know

New chapters and blank pages

bring songs and fables

and the longing for forgiveness

from past indiscretions

New chapters and blank pages

write an altered ending to an old life

where the stars shine that much brighter

on a dark night with no moon

New chapters and blank pages

bring refreshed hope for the dawning

of some passions we are forming

where we'll travel over-seas

New chapters and blank pages
allow our mind to be the vessel
for a love we've long been waiting
to uncover a buried soul

New chapters and blank pages
let us leave behind the sorrows
of what we thought we'd not see ending
in the early morning light

A Dutiful Life

A dutiful choice would not have led me to here
alone
it was not learned
but fashioned from generations of strong women
talk sent from some other place
which helped me choose this particular path

Here I journey along the
not always smooth seas
sometimes I become addicted
to the sorrow of lonely
allowing those emotions to
let the sadness ground me

It's then I realise
here is where I want to be
and the lonely sorrow is
just a dream
of a love that I've never had

Soothing words when times

were tough

the cup of tea on the table of despair

from a partner and lover

the shared concern over funds

and an empathetic arm around

tired stiff shoulders full of worry

It comes from friends

those who don't judge

don't understand or fathom me necessarily

yet who allow

the me-ness of me to flourish

those are the souls who get me through

so that as dawn breaks

I can face those mountains of yesterday

like diminished hills

and stride forward

with fortitude

gratitude

and hopefully with

a little grace

Brave Sailor

There is a brave sailor in my soul

reaching for the far horizon

hoisting the sails in my mind

trying not to be fearful of the known risks

or the unknown trip-ups that could be out there

it's Ok to make my mistakes

because we all do

and when I do

I will be strong

determined and resourceful

I will draw strength and ideas

from deep within me

that are just lying dormant in the dark

Gillie Davies

Freedom Calls

If I brought all of myself to this day

I would carry souls from years ago

to reach for a utopia yet unknown

and gift my being to the moon and stars

allow the oceans to hold me

just one more time in the vastness of life

where adventures begin and days unfold

into memories of truths yet untold

hold firm my heart

take care my soul

I will venture out once more

 freedom calls down at my core

Vital Parts of Me

Here I am

in my own piece of England

and I can move it

from shore to shore

It is here

that I have found myself

in the transient fluidity of dreams

which have built and grown

the branches of my life

I'm here knowing my choices which

have fashioned the shapes in my soul

are vital parts of me

standing my ground at peace

Gillie Davies

Shade of Human

I wasn't broken

got bent out of shape there for a while

a little rough around my edges

tender like a new shoot

twisted and squished where I didn't think

I should be

yet here I am

renewed some

replenished

bees waxed into my grain

buffed a bit too

so I'm shining a deeper shade of human

Under Blankets

I didn't join the party

didn't care to know there was one to join

I avoided cancer mates

or those who had been here before

I consciously avoided knowledge

as if that would protect me from it

I chose to hide in my own little corner of the world

and face it alone

I wonder why I did that

why I chose to isolate myself

from the physical presence of those I knew

yet chose at one point to be in the arms

of an unknown character

who wasn't interested to hear about treatment

yet who helped me hide from the demons

who hid under the blankets

Gillie Davies

Wait

The red hue

of the pre-dawn sky

speaks of wilderness

and wonder

the birds call the arrival of the day

monkeys bark and hoot

as the sea laps on the shore

a cockerel announcing the start of the day

halyards tink as the swell

rocks the boats at anchor

it's slow arriving

the dawn

making me

wait

How

Watching the world

going about its day

whilst mine has just

come crashing about my feet

earthquaked into oblivion

how do I tell mother?

Gillie Davies

Meditation

In meditation you came to me

and we walked again

through the desert

climbed the mountains

smiles and laughter

made such joyous bed fellows

in the chill of the night air

under stars of a new chapter

you took my pain

and lovingly wiped it clean

patched up the scars

smoothed salve into the blisters of sorrow

Sonnet of My Soul

I'll hold you

when your sky is black

or purple with pain

yet I'll free you to soar in the blue and gold

sing the joy of earth

and when time allows

rejoin in the greens and browns

in the quietude and bliss that

the old sailor feels

as his sails foil

when the breeze kisses the ocean

here in this moment we are all one

under the magnificent skies the universe bestows

write me a melody

that befits the picture

paint me a portrait of your beauty

and I my love will serenade

a sonnet of my soul

A Dream of Wonder

Am I still in your thoughts

or have you swept me

into a corner of dirty secrets

with your broom of shame

dare you look back

with a kind glance

to see that our passion and dreams

were love

I will come to you

in a dream of wonder

to remind you of the intense love

our souls held for each other

life was there

yours and mine

inexplicably intertwined

in moments of bliss

Ocean of Stars

Watching as the new moon sets

we marvel at the Milky Way

I watch your face

as you undress me in your mind

and naked under the stars

walk into the ocean

there you take me

again

I'm drunk with your touch

the way you kiss me

caress my soft places like they are magic

the phosphorescence sparkles as we move

making our own ocean of stars

as there you take me

again

and again

Standing Strong

Willing myself to stand tall

feeling my roots stretching out

to balance and hold

whilst you pierce me

with your words of hate

trying your best to draw blood

finding my softest points

thrusting stiletto

deep

mean

but I know what I know

my story remains mine

recognising your own vindictive cowardice

you call it mine

don't underestimate me

you will not fell me

with your lies and fallacies

I will not own your mythical story

Quietude

It is a natural quietude

in a man-made world

here where my heart lives

has a depth

a serenity

unhindered

untouched by man

Gillie Davies

Risked to Be

The years have flown by
sitting here I watch
as people rush through their lives
just as I did as a young woman
as if
there is more to it than what they have

In my aloneness
I am content to be in this life
that is all there is
no elixir for continued youth
as if youth were the pinnacle

Old age is the apex
to have reached it at all a miracle
I love the lines etched in my skin
they show that I laughed
I loved
I risked to be

Empty Spaces

There's no one here at the moment

fans creak and whine moving the air

in empty spaces

yet to be filled with

laughter or sadness

Dusty with age and lack of use

spiders work their miracles with silks

waiting momentarily for life to return

Empress Queen

The first hit

like a bullet through the eye

standing tall

shoulders back

chin high

still

swallow

breathe

swallow

blink

calms her mind

allowing the words to penetrate

some just drift away

can't take them in

holds herself

silently calling her inner woman

professional to the end

they cannot see anything but strength

so strong in this her vulnerability

she disempowers them with it

empowers all the small people

such grace

holding her orb

nothing can touch her

she is Empress Queen

Gillie Davies

Depression

It doesn't look as you'd expect

it is dirty

dusty

with old skin and hair

an unmade bed

unwiped surface

dishes in the sink

it is tired and weary worn

down at heal

unkempt

listless and lethargic

without thought for a second glance

It stays at home

hides away from the world

keeps quiet

alone

dark in its place

not seeing

not caring

oblivious to its own destruction

caring

yet not caring to care

tired

so damned tired

It is wrinkled and wrecked

as a ship sunk at sea

lying in its place

allowing the dead

the dying

to rest on the surface

until the whole

is disappeared beneath it

smothering all life

vitality

joy

under sharp coral

silted up

to rot in the depths

It's not glamorous

pretty

celebrity nor bold

its distant

cold

dismantled

impaired

it touches like acid

and arrives from nowhere

without announcement

or appointment

and cuts

as a machete

no grace

no favour

Out of Chaos

I watched the perfect cloud

drift and stretch across the morning sky

dusted pink with the coming dawn

over a glittering sea

and I wondered

what dream is this I see

out of chaos and destruction

from the turmoil

comes peace

Gillie Davies

Life is Beating

Here in the dawn

the sea otter watches as the winter sun

claws her way

up the mountainside

to pop her sunny smile

over the top and bring warmth

to the lonely traveller

Eagles call to their young

feeding on today's catch of sea snake and whiting

under the grey clouds

which write a story

of North Sea storms and mountainous waves

chilling memory of life to the bone

Deep in the forest

branches creek in applause

as one finally releases its grip

cascading in a cacophony of shrieks

landing on the soft bed

of broken leaf dreams

which floated to their deaths

in chilly autumn winds

Hear the breath that monkeys sigh

the lions roar

camels and the rhinos' snort

frog and gecko croak

these proclaim there is life

still beating in

the soul of our mother earth

Gillie Davies

The Woman

I met the woman

from my past

we spoke of things

that didn't last

women in colours

different hues

of old familiars

said nothing new

told our stories

of each other

the gifts and hurts

new friends

old lovers

and soon the time

it came to part

to walk different ways

down altered paths

and now I see

what I was shown

were just the seeds

my steps had sown

I may yet meet her

once again

I wonder if

she'll know me then

will I regret

things I have told

to those who follow

the way so cold

or will I know

I cannot change

the writings

on another's page

will this woman

who I once was

forgive my errors

reprieve my loss

will she smile

and set me free

to think my thoughts

and let me be

Distinguished

Right Whales are distinguished

from the other

baleen whales

by their very long baleen

Right!

with an almost silky texture

the bristles feed

small planktonic crustaceans

mainly copepods

Right!

Whales are distinguished

Gillie Davies

Shock

It's the shock of it that gets to me

it's tiny but not supposed to be there

like a small alien implant

had I been brave enough

I would have cut it out the moment I found it

but

It's the shock of it that gets to me

Then the confirmation that it was there

like I needed confirmation!

it's my body I know about it

It's the shock of it that gets to me

after the squishing and the probing and prodding

the confirmation

and it's the shock of it that gets to me

The removal was smooth enough

like living outside myself

just watching the process

sleep-walking through it all

but

it's the shock of it that gets to me

the scars are there

bigger than expected it grew so fast

yet

it's the shock of it that gets to me

Therapy is upon me now

and it's the shock of it that gets to me

not the scanning or blood tests

nor even the injection

that makes my body feel its presence

through my veins

like hot milk mixing with my blood

it's the shock of it that gets to me

Now it's almost done and dusted

but the burning is getting worse

and it's the shock of it that gets to me

my skin so parched and sore

the tenderness where it takes its toll

and really at the end of it

it's the shock of it that gets to me

in the darkness on my own

Brighter Tomorrow

For a depression or sadness

sometimes there is no why

but that's Ok

I hear the weariness in your words

being world weary is no fun

I get that too

All those people you hold

know the feeling too

but just can't say the words

Hold on my friend there is a sun

over that far horizon there are stars shining

above those clouds of fear doubt and weariness

Let's sit a while together in silence

watch the sun rise

on that brighter tomorrow

Gillie Davies

A Penny

Did you ever stop to wonder
about the people you squandered
with gossip and your meanness
with your show-pony attitude
prancing out in finery
pretending to be proper
did it give you a little confidence
to twist the knife again?

Now the days are drawing darker
and you age from bitter spite
mouth is twisted a sharp thin line
your money buys you things
while people around you die
for want of just a penny in their tin
go on with what your life has been
keep up appearances and distance
I see the shallow pool of water
in which you hide

Storms

The veil of stormy thoughts lifts

and even if the fear felt real

the sun was always shining

behind the shadows of misapprehension

the protection you seek is within you

it has always been so

the stars are in your veins my darling

they will never let go

Cyclonic Fall-out

The creaking of the spars a reminder of sorts

as we rolled in the swell of emotional trauma

under heavy leaded skies of anxiety and disquiet

anticipating harsh realities of cyclonic fall out

that it could have been avoided

had we trodden the familiar path of millions

not selected the route where risk was inevitable

I watch you in the cinematography

smiling and waving

such joy and abandonment as if forever was ours

but our time was tidal

driven by the moon passing overhead

we could not know

that our love would be drowned in the monsoon

of judgemental piety

by those who break joy

like the stem of a flower

Obsession

Obsession

smelled sweet

a heady colour

from dawn 'til dusk

Jealousy

cut me

from your heart

turning wine to poison

Destruction

broken walls

raising the dust

of long dead souls

Resurrection

Gillie Davies

Deep Blue

In the deep blue

where sky and sea meet

I'll wait for you

in the bliss of my seclusion

with a heart full of loving

my head full of melodies

and my soul singing love songs

Bitter Taste

I think it was in that moment

I realised you were gone

when the bitter taste of truth

drenched my lips

with the poison of others

who had told you a story

their truths not ours

their lies not our joys

the slow rolling motion

from the ocean swell

takes my mind back

to a more gentle time

when the importance of the day

was for water and food and safety afloat

I believe we were happy then

living the adventure of our lives

loving each other completely

in a bubble all our own

Gillie Davies

New Place

Here is a new place

in between the lives of small islands

and the souls of trees

where blue-birds and insects take flight

on a mythical exploration

of dreams

floating on yesterday's knowledge

in the ocean of words

the silence of nature

sings its melody for

all who care to listen

yes listen

to the cry of the eagle

proclaiming

its place in the

world of lost thoughts

Bear Witness

Did you dare to dream so boldly

as to achieve strength and knowing

beyond where your eyes looked

or did you realise all too late

that your own self sabotage

ripped the golden orb from your grasp

Heed not what another tells

is unachievable for you

take your dream in all its preposterousness

and polish it daily with self-belief

until suddenly you arrive

almost unnoticeably

at the door of personal growth and peace

having trodden a path so unique

that only you can bear witness to it

Gillie Davies

Dance 'til Dawn

In the breathless evening

the imam calls his faithful to prayer

and the new moon

in the cloudless sky

speaks of her intentions

to touch my soul

and dance with it until the dawn

Thinking Differently

Feel the early morning crispness

caress smiling cheeks

touch the tingling fingers with excitement

under the warmth of the day

clean in the new clarity of thoughts

lifted from a refreshing brew of ideas

laughing through the mind

like birdsong

to start taking new risks

in thinking differently

Shallow Breathing

There are times
when my soul feels tired to its core
I have to focus on placing little washers
on the bolts that hold me together
otherwise
it just all gets too much

Some bolts are in very hard to get to places
and the fingers of my mind altogether too clumsy
it takes patience
hours and hours of concentration

All the time
the shallow breathing is starving me
of the loving arms of oxygen
so I have to stop and focus on my breathing

I repeat this all day

until I fall into the oblivion of sleep

then

I could sleep for a thousand years

Gillie Davies

Addicted to Sorrow

Some days it feels like I am addicted

to the sweet-smelling nectar of sorrow

tears stream down like rivulets of rain

from the leaves of my being

Gathering in a pool at my feet

I watch in the silence of the morning

as the joy and freedom

the laughter and childlike thrill of life

melt into the puddle

Yet I so wish

I could feel the happiness that was there

where did it go

what have I become

a pitiful addict to suffering

loss and pain

At Anchor

At anchor

I watch the other boats

with their comings and goings

friends arriving

leaving

passing by

all turn in harmony with the tide

none too close

anchor lights start to burn

sunset magnificent

a blessing to be at anchor

Droplets

Can you see

where the droplets of your words

lay puddled on my skin

not yet soaking in

Did you know

that sometimes I just lie still

until they have seeped right in

becoming mine

Are we one then

as I gaze over at your thoughts

hovering above my head

like a small rain cloud of misgiving

Shall we dance

amongst the tears of lovers' past

a slow lamenting gyration

through night until dawn

Little Print

I want to leave

a little print of kindness

on someone's heart

in the shape of me

for perhaps it will be

my only legacy

Just to be

How would it be

just to be

to allow myself

to stand in this space

not wishing I was someone else

or in some other place

to know what I know

without judgement or apprehension

to look at the world

without wondering

if I could have been better

Gift

Unexpectedness landed at my feet

all wrapped up

so I couldn't see

its preciousness initially

yet as I sat here with it

peeling off layers of unease

I started to realise how monumental

this chaotically wrapped gift

was to me

Acknowledgements

I would like to say an extra special thank you to: -

Dennison Berwick: *Author and fellow sailor, for continuing to encourage me and chase away my black dog!*

Tim Stone: *Photographer who generously allowed me to use his exquisite photographs*

Ranajit Paul of RGraphic: *My graphic designer who took an idea, made it real, put up with my constant change of heart and finally produced this beautiful book cover.*

Frances Garner: *Ocean Sailor and dear friend of many years for reading and discussing this book and holding me gently when I need it.*

Jan Castle: *Life Coach, Poet, Leader and friend who runs a wonderful course which started in the 2020 pandemic called "The Write Space" it is an absolute lifeline.*

Celeste Cicchini: *- A beautiful soul and sailor who gave up her time to proof read whilst sitting at anchor in quarantine in Thailand!*

Feaky Abdullah: *- An exquisite being whose joy and laughter as well as some proof reading got me to the print stage.*

Angela Davies: *- My mother, to whom I am indebted on so many levels and who I love dearly.*

Other Books in the Series

Solo Sailing the South China Sea

A poetry anthology from life afloat. Imagine living on a small boat, sailing the oceans of the world, having love, losing it, feeling alone and occasionally lonely and delving into your heart and soul to find answers through verse. A woman bobbing about on her little boat, creating inspiring and insightful thoughts and putting them to paper, this is the first of several poetry books, describing the feelings and thoughts of a Solo Sailing Woman.

Solo Sailing the Andaman Sea

This is the second in a series of 5 books of Biographical poetry, written by a Solo Yachtswoman circumnavigating the world's Oceans. A memoir of sorts, where the writer explores her emotions, dreams, inspirations, fears and tribulations as she negotiates the sometimes hostile, sometimes idyllic waters of the world, whilst often self isolating. These words take one on a journey with the writer where the adventures are so real that the emotions rage within one as if one is there! This is a series of brave encounters and courage to face the unknown alone on a small boat in the ocean, where when things go wrong, there is just one woman alone to deal with it. Many have found courage to follow their own dreams from reading these insightful words.

Future Books in the Series

Solo Sailing the Indian Ocean

This will be a collection of poems leading up to and including crossing the Indian Ocean alone. Gillie anticipates it taking 2.5months non-stop sailing to Tanzania.

Solo Sailing to the Moon

In this the final book in the series Gillie intends to take some of your favourites from across the years, Seas and Oceans and add some little anecdotes along the way. Recalling some memories of passed voyages and people who have blessed her adventurous life.

INDEX OF FIRST LINE

www.ingramcontent.com/pod-product-compliance
Lightning Source LLC
Chambersburg PA
CBHW031135090426
42738CB00008B/1090